MY CONTRIBUTION TOWARDS WORLD PEACE

DR. BINOD KUMAR SINHA

Contents

Dr. Binod Kumar Sinha

Dr. Binod Kumar Sinha born on 12 February 1934 is a multidimensional personality who has been a helping hand to society over the past decades. After passing their B.Sc., Dr. Sinha joined St. Michaels High School, Patna, and he served there for

2 years, being an advocate he has been honored with many prestigious awards like the limca book of records, the great citizen of Bihar, the siksha Ratna award, siksha Bhushan award, national child care development award, vidhi Ratna award and many more.

He has also written more than 16books which are very influential that are

Fight against poverty

- Extract of life
- Problems of the unemployed
- Let us empower women
- Tales of noble prize winners
- Know and grow with the stock market
- Tales From Bible
- Know and Protect your Fundamental Rights
- Tales From Quran
- FIGHT AGAINST WATER POLLUTION
- Illiterate Children's
- How to become a successful Lawyer
- SWASTH RAHKAR LAMBI UMAR KAISE PAYEIN
- Fight Against Air Pollution
- FIGHT AGAINST WOMEN'S SOCIAL HARASSMENT
- FIGHT AGAINST SUICIDE AND DEPRESSION
- Stories Of lord Buddha
- Fight Against Hunger
- Problems of Senior Citizens and their solution
- Fight against Child trafficking
- Biography of Dr. Binod Kumar Sinha
- The insight Of Bhagwad Geeta
- Fight against Poverty
- The Covid 19
- Extract of life
- Tales from Bhagwatam
- Problems of the unemployed
- Let us empower women
- Tales of a noble prize winner

DR. BINOD KUMAR SINHA

Peace

Peace is a concept of societal friendship and harmony without hostility and violence. In a social sense, peace is commonly used to mean a lack of conflict (such as war) and freedom from fear of violence between individuals or groups. Throughout history, leaders have used peacemaking and diplomacy to establish a type of behavioral restraint that has resulted in regional peace or economic growth through various forms of agreements or peace treaties. Such

behavioral restraint has often resulted in reduced conflict, greater economic interactivity, and consequently substantial prosperity.

"Psychological peace" (such as peaceful thinking and emotions) is perhaps less well defined, yet often a necessary precursor to establishing "behavioral peace." Friendly behavior sometimes results from a "peaceful inner disposition." Some have expressed the belief that peace can be initiated with a certain quality of inner tranquility that does not depend upon the uncertainties of daily life. The acquisition of such a "peaceful internal disposition" for oneself and others can contribute to resolving otherwise seemingly irreconcilable competing interests. Peace is not a state of excitement although we are happy when excited, peace is when one's mind is quiet and satisfied.

The term 'peace' originates most recently from the Anglo-French pes, and the Old French pais, meaning "peace, reconciliation, silence, the agreement" (11th century).The Anglo-French term pes itself comes from the Latin pax, meaning "peace, compact, agreement, treaty of peace, tranquility, absence of hostility, harmony." The English word came into use in various personal greetings from c. 1300 as a translation of the Hebrew word shalom, which, according to Jewish theology, comes from a Hebrew verb meaning 'to be complete, whole'.[5] Although 'peace' is the usual translation, however, it is an incomplete one, because 'shalom,' which is also cognate with the Arabic salaam, has multiple other meanings in addition to peace, including justice, good health, safety, well-being, prosperity, equity, security, good fortune, and friendliness, as well as simply the greetings, "hello" and "goodbye".[6] On a personal level, peaceful behaviors are kind, considerate, respectful, just, and tolerant of others' beliefs and behaviors – tending to manifest goodwill.

This latter understanding of peace can also pertain to an individual's introspective sense or concept of her/himself, as in being "at peace" in one's own mind, as found in European references from c. 1200. The early English term is also used in the sense of "quiet", reflecting calm, serene, and meditative approaches to family or group relationships that avoid quarreling and seek tranquility — an absence of disturbance or agitation.

In many languages, the word for peace is also used as a greeting or a farewell, for example, the Hawaiian word aloha, as well as the Arabic word salaam. In English, the word peace is occasionally used as a farewell, especially for the dead, as in the phrase rest in peace.

Wolfgang Dietrich, in his research project which led to the book The Palgrave International Handbook of Peace Studies (2011), maps the different meanings of peace in different languages and regions across the world. Later, in his Interpretations of Peace in History and Culture (2012), he groups the different meanings of peace into five peace families: Energetic/Harmony,

Moral/Justice, Modern/Security, Postmodern/Truth, and Transrational, a synthesis of the positive sides of the four previous families and the society.

• 4 •

In ancient times and more recently, peaceful alliances between different nations were codified through royal marriages. Two examples, Hermodike I (c. 800 BC)[7] and Hermodike II (c. 600 BC)[8] were Greek princesses from the house of Agamemnon who married kings from what is now Central Turkey. The union of Phrygia / Lydia with Aeolian Greeks resulted in regional peace, which facilitated the transfer of ground-breaking technological skills into Ancient Greece; respectively, the phonetic written script and the minting of coinage (to use a token currency, where the value is guaranteed by the state).[9] Both inventions were rapidly adopted by surrounding nations through further trade and cooperation and have been of fundamental benefit to the progress of civilization.

Throughout history, victors have sometimes used ruthless measures to impose peace upon the vanquished. In his book Agricola, the Roman historian Tacitus includes eloquent and vicious polemics against the rapacity and greed of Rome. One, that Tacitus says is by the Caledonian chieftain Calgacus, ends with: Auferre trucidare rapere falsis nominibus imperium, atque ubi solitudinem faciunt, pacem appellant. (To ravage, to slaughter, to usurp under false titles, they call empire; and where they make a desert, they call it peace. — Oxford Revised Translation).

Discussion of peace is therefore at the same time a discussion on its form.. Is it simply the absence of mass organized killing (war), or does peace require a particular morality and justice? (just peace). Peace must be seen at least in two forms:

A simple silence of arms, absence of war.

The absence of war is accompanied by particular requirements for the mutual settlement of relations, which are characterized by terms such as justice, mutual respect, respect for the law, and goodwill.

More recently, advocates for radical reform in justice systems have called for a public policy adoption of non-punitive, non-violent Restorative Justice methods. Many of those studying the success of these methods, including a United Nations working group on Restorative Justice Archived 26 July 2011 at the Wayback Machine, have attempted to re-define justice in terms related to peace. From the late 2000s on, a Theory of Active Peace has been proposed that conceptually integrates justice into a larger peace theory.

Another internationally important approach to peace is the international, national and local protection of cultural assets in the event of conflicts. United Nations, UNESCO, and Blue Shield International deal with the protection of cultural heritage. This also applies to the integration of United Nations peacekeeping. UNESCO Director-General Irina Bokova stated: "The protection of culture and heritage is a humanitarian and security policy imperative that also paves the way for resilience, reconciliation, and peace." The protection of cultural heritage should preserve the particularly sensitive cultural memory, the growing cultural diversity, and the economic basis of a state, a municipality, or a region. In many conflicts, there is a deliberate attempt to destroy the opponent's cultural heritage. Whereby there is also a connection between cultural user disruption or cultural heritage and the cause of flight. However, protection can only be implemented in a sustainable manner through the fundamental cooperation and training of military units and civilian personnel, together with the locals. The president of Blue Shield International Karl von Habsburg summed it up with the words: "Without the local community and without the local participants, that would be completely impossible".

There are three simple solutions to peace. The three solutions are, eliminating war, communication, and respecting people's differences. Many of our loved ones have died in wars. And regardless of where one is from, we can all agree that death is a tragedy that can be avoided. Soldiers are risking their lives and leaving families in fear wondering whether or not they will return home safely. There is a vast amount of people from various countries who have no food or shelter. Meanwhile, we are disputing over unnecessary topics such as race, money, and cultural differences, which leads to war! People should not be judged by who they are, what they have, or what they believe in. For instance, I am a 12 year old who has to cope with and accept my disability of being blind. I wouldn't want people to judge me for only that. I am no different than anyone else. Everyone needs to put forth an effort to communicate in order to avoid conflict. Without communication, it would be very challenging to come together as one, and promote world peace. It takes a team effort to make the world a peaceful place. It's encouraging how the world works together in a synergistic union to make the world part of a more peaceful universe. If we don't respect people's differences, then we can't have peace. You can't just look at somebody and judge them because they are different. For example, if your best friend suddenly became terminally ill, offer them moral support and try to see things through their perspective. This might inspire you to treat them more equally. Most people who are different are more aware with their other senses. I am blind. However, I have senses that make me see a clear vision for world peace. I can hear the laughter of families floating across the borders of all countries. Laughter and communication skills are universal languages. I can taste the various foods from across the globe, blending seamlessly together, making their way to the less fortunate. I can smell the clean air from everywhere knowing that everyone needs air to breath and would enjoy feasting on the various aromas weaved throughout the world. Most importantly, I can feel the sense and feel the power of peace when I meet a stranger and offer a peaceful greeting without being judgmental. People are different. People have much to offer, whether it be an act of kindness or discovering a cure for an illness. Joined together, different types of people are a powerful force and could inspire the world to function more successfully and peacefully. I may be blind, but I have the power to promote peacefulness on a daily basis. All the things that I have mentioned should be practiced on a daily basis. If we all put our best foot forward, then the world would be a better place. So, as you can see, if we try to avoid wars, communicate more, and respect people's differences, we would have a more peaceful environment.

Peacekeepers

Police

The obligation of the state to provide for domestic peace within its borders in usually charged to the police and other general domestic policing activities. The police are a constituted body of persons empowered by a state to enforce the law, protect citizens' lives, liberty, and possessions, and prevent crime and civil disorder. Their powers include the power of arrest and the legitimized use of force. The term is most commonly associated with the police forces of a sovereign state that are authorized to exercise the police power of that state within a defined legal or territorial area of responsibility. Police forces are often defined as being separate from the military and other organizations involved in the defense of the state against foreign aggressors; however, the gendarmerie is a military unit charged with civil policing.[19] Police forces are usually public sector services, funded through taxes.

National security

It is the obligation of national security to providing for peace and security in a nation against foreign threats and foreign aggression. Potential causes of national insecurity include actions by other states (e.g. military or cyber attack), violent non-state actors (e.g. terrorist attack), organized criminal groups such as narcotic cartels, and also the effects of natural disasters (e.g. flooding, earthquakes).: v, 1–8 Systemic drivers of insecurity, which may be transnational, include climate change, economic inequality and marginalization, political exclusion, and militarization.[In view of the wide range of risks, the preservation of peace and the security of a nation-state have several dimensions, including economic security, energy security, physical security, environmental security, food security, border security, and cyber security. These dimensions correlate closely with elements of national power.

League of Nations

The principal forerunner of the United Nations was the League of Nations. It was created at the Paris Peace Conference of 1919 and emerged from the advocacy of Woodrow Wilson and other idealists during World War I. The Covenant of the League of Nations was included in the Treaty of Versailles in 1919. The League was based in Geneva until its dissolution as a result of World War II and its replacement by the United Nations. The high hopes widely held for the League in the 1920s, for example amongst members of the League of Nations Union, gave way to widespread disillusion in the 1930s as the League struggled to respond to challenges from Nazi Germany, Fascist Italy, and Japan.

One of the most important scholars of the League of Nations was Sir Alfred Eckhard Zimmern. Like many of the other British enthusiasts for the League, such as Gilbert Murray and Florence Stawell – known as the "Greece and peace" set – he came to this from the study of the classics.

The creation of the League of Nations, and the hope for informed public opinion on international issues (expressed for example by the Union for Democratic Control during World War I), also saw the creation after World War I of bodies dedicated to understanding international affairs, such as the Council on Foreign Relations in New York and the Royal Institute of International Affairs at Chatham House in London. At the same time, the academic study of international relations started to professionalize, with the creation of the first professorship of international politics, named for Woodrow Wilson, at Aberystwyth, Wales, in 1919.

Olympic Games

The late 19th-century idealist advocacy of peace which led to the creation of the Nobel Peace Prize, the Rhodes Scholarships, the Carnegie Endowment for International Peace, and ultimately the League of Nations, also saw the re-emergence of the ancient Olympic ideal. Led by Pierre de Coubertin, this culminated in the holding of 1896 of the first of the modern Olympic Games.

Nobel Peace Prize

Henry Dunant was awarded the first-ever Nobel Peace Prize for his role in founding the International Red Cross.

The highest honor awarded to peacemakers is the Nobel Prize in Peace, awarded in 1901 by the Norwegian Nobel Committee. It is awarded annually to internationally notable persons following the prize's creation in the will of Alfred Nobel. According to Nobel's will, the Peace Prize shall be awarded to the person who "...shall have done the most or the best work for fraternity between nations, for the abolition or reduction of standing armies, and for the holding and promotion of peace congresses.

Rhodes, Fulbright, and Schwarzman scholarships

In creating the Rhodes Scholarships for outstanding students from the United States, Germany, and much of the British Empire, Cecil Rhodes wrote in 1901 that 'the object is that an understanding between the three great powers will render war impossible and educational relations make the strongest tie'. This peace purpose of the Rhodes Scholarships was very prominent in the first half of the 20th century and became prominent again in recent years under Warden of the Rhodes House Donald Markwell, a historian of thought about the causes of war and peace This vision greatly influenced Senator J. William Fulbright in the goal of the Fulbright fellowships to promote international understanding and peace, and has guided many other international fellowship programs, including the Schwarzman Scholars to China created by Stephen A. Schwarzman in 2013.

Gandhi Peace Prize

Mahatma Gandhi.

The International Gandhi Peace Prize, named after Mahatma Gandhi, is awarded annually by the Government of India. It was launched as a tribute to the ideals espoused by Gandhi in 1995 on the occasion of the 125ᵗʰ anniversary of his birth. This is an annual award given to individuals and institutions for their contributions towards social, economic, and political transformation through non-violence and other Gandhian methods. The award carries Rs. 10 million in cash, convertible in any currency in the world, a plaque, and a citation. It is open to all persons regardless of nationality, race, creed, or sex.

Student Peace Prize

The Student Peace Prize is awarded biennially to a student or a student organization that has significantly contributed to promoting peace and human rights.

Ahmadiyya Muslim Peace Prize

The Ahmadiyya Muslim Peace Prize is awarded annually "in recognition of an individual's or an organization's contribution to the advancement of the cause of peace". The prize was first launched in 2009 by the Ahmadiyya Muslim Peace Prize Committee under the directive of the caliph of the Ahmadiyya Muslim Community, Mirza Masroor Ahmad.

Culture of Peace News Network

The Culture of Peace News Network, otherwise known simply as CPNN, is an UN-authorized interactive online news network, committed to supporting the global movement for a culture of peace.

Rainbows: Often used as a symbol of harmony and peace.

Sydney Peace Prize

Every year in the first week of November, the Sydney Peace Foundation presents the Sydney Peace Prize. The Sydney Peace Prize is awarded to an organization or an individual whose life and work has demonstrated significant contributions to:
The achievement of peace with justice locally, nationally or internationally
The promotion and attainment of human rights

The philosophy, language, and practice of non-violence

Museums

A peace museum is a museum that documents historical peace initiatives. Many provide advocacy programs for nonviolent conflict resolution. This may include conflicts at the personal, regional or international level.

Smaller institutions include the Randolph Bourne Institute, the McGill Middle East Program of Civil Society and Peace Building, and the International Festival of Peace Poetry. Considering current developments and transformations in the world, the role of UN organs in maintaining and strengthening the international peace and security shall be properly addressed, as the political, military, economic, ecological and social environment in which the UN operates today has changed considerably and continues to evolve. Presently the range of global threats and challenges to international peace and security is multifold and includes, inter alia, threats from poverty, disease, and environmental degradation (the threats to human security), threats from conflict between states, threats from violence and massive human rights violations within states, threats from terrorism, organized crime, threats from the proliferation of weapons - particularly WMD. As regards conflicts, in particular inter-state ones, Chapter VI of the Charter of the United Nations requires parties to any dispute that threatens international peace and security to negotiate or use other peaceful means to resolve their conflict. While the organization has ensured that no world war has taken place since its formation, however the criticism of UN capacity to deal with issues related to international peace and security has increased, which can be explained in relation to its modes of operation. Today we are witnessing the looming demise of the security architecture which certainly has not started just recently, during the last couple of months. We felt the shatter of multilateralism, the crack of international institutions and disrespect for fundamental rules less than two years ago when Azerbaijan, abandoning the peaceful negotiations and violating the principle of non-use of force, unleashed a war against Nagorno Karabakh and its people. The right to self-determination has been one of the main purposes of the United Nations and use of force against this right can trigger an entire chain of human rights violations including mass atrocities and ethnic cleansing. This is something we observe during and after the war initiated by Azerbaijan. The military aggression in September-November 2020 was the practical display of the continued Azerbaijani intention to seek a military solution to the Nagorno Karabakh conflict, to use force. Azerbaijani authorities were threatening to use force very consistently over past years, which was combined with a bellicose rhetoric. Both Armenia and Nagorno Karabakh have always been very explicit in that there is no alternative to the peaceful settlement of the conflict. There are undeniable facts that it is Azerbaijan who initiated this aggression. For years Azerbaijan has consistently violated the 1994-1995 agreements on the establishment of ceasefire regime, which have no time limitation, has been rejecting the proposals of the OSCE Minsk Group Co-Chairmanship on introducing investigation mechanisms of ceasefire violations and the strengthening of the ceasefire monitoring, thus retaining the possibilities of the use of force. On 23 March 2020, the UN Secretary-General issued an urgent appeal for a global ceasefire in all corners of the world, by emphasizing that people suffering in conflict zones are particularly vulnerable to the pandemic. The UN High Commissioner for Human Rights also underscored the direct threat of wars during the pandemic to public health and lives. In July 2020, the UN Security Council adopted Resolution S/RES/2532 (2020) and expressed grave concern about the devastating impact of the COVID-19 pandemic across the world, especially in countries ravaged by armed conflicts, or in postconflict situations, or affected by humanitarian crises. It recognized that conditions of violence and instability in conflict situations can exacerbate the pandemic, and that inversely the pandemic can exacerbate the adverse humanitarian impact of conflict situations. Thus, the Security Council demanded a general and immediate cessation of hostilities in all situations, called upon all parties to armed conflicts to engage immediately in a durable humanitarian pause. 180 countries, regional organizations, civil society groups, peace advocates and millions of global citizens have also endorsed the ceasefire call. Despite all this,

Azerbaijan launched a wide-scale aggressive war against Nagorno Karabakh during the global pandemic, in opposition to a call for global ceasefire by the UN Secretary-General and the demand of the UN Security Council for a general and immediate cessation of hostilities in all situations. The aim was to create an epidemiological disaster in Nagorno Karabakh, accelerate the rapid spread of the deadly virus, to achieve the eventual collapse of the health care system, causing increased deaths, other serious injuries and great sufferings to the population. This offensive policy was accompanied with the use of banned weapons against civilians and civilian infrastructure, use of explosive weapons in populated areas and mass displacement of the population, further deteriorating the pandemic situation. The Azerbaijani armed forces attacked more than 130 civilian objects, including densely populated ones, as well as schools, kindergartens, maternity hospital, with aerial, artillery, rocket and tank fire strikes and cluster munitions, most of which were targeted or indiscriminate, killing and injuring civilians. In the cases of indiscriminate attacks, the Azerbaijani forces failed to abide by the obligation to distinguish between military targets and civilians. Nor did they take feasible precautions to minimize harm to civilians. In many cases, attacking the civilians was targeted and intentional, since military targets were located very far from the civilian objects. The absence of military targets in the vicinity of attacks further confirms their deliberate nature, which amounts to a war crime. Actions were carried out by Azerbaijan also against the sovereign territory of the Republic of Armenia, targeting the civilian population and non-military infrastructure, as a result of which there were casualties among the Armenian population, as well as serious material damages to the housing stock and social institutions. Attacks on journalists by Azerbaijani forces occurred in several instances, in violation of Article 79 of Protocol I of the Geneva Conventions, which states that journalists engaged in professional work in war zones "shall be considered as civilians" and "shall be protected as such under the Conventions and this Protocol, provided that they take no action adversely affecting their status as civilians.". Among a number of war crimes against civilians of Nagorno Karabakh, there were a number of severe violations recorded against tangible and intangible cultural heritage, including religious. During the months of the war and nowadays videos and photos made by Azerbaijani soldiers being proud of fully "taking revenge" from the historical monuments, cross stones, memorials across the territories of Azerbaijani appearance in Nagorno Karabakh, are numerous. Azerbaijanis express particular aggression against those historical monuments that have Armenian inscriptions or crosses. Though a number of specialized international organisations have made statements condemning and calling on the importance of the protection of the cultural heritage by referring to the UN Resolution 2347 on the protection of the cultural heritage located in the conflict zones adopted in 2017, we still witness gross violations as against humans, particularly war prisoners, so the religious and cultural heritage of the Armenians of Nagorno Karabakh, which can be referred to as the Cultural Genocide, the aim of which is to erase the historical traces of the memory of the annihilated indigenous population. Therefore, today it is imperative to save the thousands of cultural, including religious monuments under the Azerbaijani control in Nagorno Karabakh. Azerbaijan, as a state party to the Geneva Conventions is obliged to take all the measures under the mentioned treaties to secure all rights provided for both prisoners of war and civilian persons. Moreover, those norms also constitute part of customary international law and must be abided by as part of general international law. However, contrary to its obligations under IHL norms Azerbaijan and its agents have been engaged in violent and inhuman treatment of those captured. Unjustifiable delay in the repatriation of prisoners of war or civilians also constitutes a grave breach of IHL. The regime of IHL persists and applies with respect to both civilians and combatants that have been kidnapped or taken hostage by the Azerbaijani forces after the November 9 Statement of 2020. The captivation of civilians can also qualify as enforced disappearance which is prohibited under customary international law. Currently, Azerbaijan has confirmed holding of only 38 Armenian prisoners of war and captive civilians (out of 38 persons 35 are servicemen, and 3 are civilians). All these people have been sentenced to various years of imprisonment according to the decisions made by the Azerbaijani court. The criminal cases against the captured Armenians have no legal basis and contradict international legal norms. The fundamental right to a fair trial is violated. The whole process of criminal prosecution based on fabricated charges and accusations against prisoners of war and civilian captives is accompanied by the violation of the fundamental right to a fair trial. Armenian prisoners of war and civilians taken hostage are subjected to torture and ill-treatment. Numerous cases of killing of captives and enforced disappearances have been recorded. The provisional measures put forward by the International Court of Justice on December 7, 2021 which instruct Azerbaijan to cease racist and discriminatory policies against Armenians including destruction and vandalism of the Armenian cultural heritage should be unconditionally implemented. These measures come to prove the anti-Armenian policies of Azerbaijan including its bellicose rhetoric, depriving the people of their means of subsistence, constantly terrorizing Armenian population and threatening with new use of force. Azerbaijan continues to put a siege on Nagorno Karabakh impeding the access of the international humanitarian organizations, including those who requested a fact-finding mission to determine the state of cultural heritage. The UN and its bodies have been bestowed with a universal mandate to enjoy unconditional, unimpeded, unhindered access to the people in need, wherever they are and in all circumstances. Thus, the international community, and in particular UN, has to assume responsibility for ensuring unconditional access to the whole territory of Nagorno Karabakh. The UN Special Procedure Mandate Holders issued several communications to Azerbaijan raising questions with regard to the use of mercenaries, extrajudicial executions, arbitrary detentions, enforced disappearances, destruction of religious and cultural heritage in the context of the Nagorno Karabakh conflict. Azerbaijan declined to give a proper response to these communications, in a sheer defiance to the UN Human rights machinery. The impunity leads to new violations. Apart from Nagorno Karabakh, Azerbaijan continues its policy of human rights abuses now on the borderline areas of the Republic of Armenia, wherein the civilian population suffers from constant provocative actions of armed forces of Azerbaijan. This aggressive policy is accompanied by the overt violations of international humanitarian law. Overall, the international reaction to Azerbaijan's war crimes in Nagorno Karabakh has been largely inactive and even indifferent. Generic calls on both sides under the circumstances when Armenia makes credible steps towards peace, while Azerbaijan continues the escalation of the situation, may indicate indifference and lack of commitment from our international partners. If we want to reach stability in the region then there is no other way for the international community than being frank on these issues, without applying double standards. 2) What solutions to you deem necessary to overcome those challenges? Security sector governance has been a key element on the UN agenda to sustain peace and prevent the outbreak, escalation, continuation and recurrence of conflicts. On 3 December 2020, the UN Security Council unanimously adopted resolution 2553, reaffirming the importance of security sector reform in peacebuilding, and sustaining peace, including conflict prevention and in the stabilization and reconstruction of States in the aftermath of conflict. One of the solutions to overcome the challenges to maintaining and strengthening international peace and security may be the security sector governance reform, which may, however, be a complex and long-term endeavor. The UN conflict risk assessment mechanism in terms of an early detection of a worsening situation might be improved as the risk assessment is a strong tool to identify significant risks in order to integrate risk management measures or enhance and adjust responses - and response planning - accordingly. The deteriorating human rights practices and non-observance of internationally recognized human rights standards, lack of progress in ensuring greater democracy in Azerbaijan were the clear signals of the impending instigation of the war by the latter. Proper addressing of human rights violations as potential precursors of atrocity crimes and conflict shall be duly in place for conflict-affected areas, states engaged in the conflict or being at risk of a potential involvement. Human rights violations are often the clearest indications of a looming conflict. A comprehensive and common analysis of the human rights situation and conflict drivers will enable the Organization to take system-wide actions to prevent greater violations from occurring. The revision of UN-specific post-conflict response and peacebuilding practices and procedures in terms of a timely provision of response measures might be conducted, as the existing procedures are too long and time-consuming. The international community and UN in particular should be very explicit in its statements and clear in its attitudes as to which party has breached or is breaching international obligations and human rights. It is necessary to name the violations of human rights exactly as they are, and there is no need to put an equality sign between the parties as it is sometimes done by political actors. For example, the UN should be more honest in its public statements and policy when the issue is about immediate repatriation of prisoners of war, as well as manifestations of discrimination and hate speech (for instance against Armenians by high-ranking officials of Azerbaijan). There are ample mechanisms to call a State that is a serial violator of human rights to order, and thus to avert yet another.

CHAPTER THREE

How to maintain Peace

Pacifism is the categorical opposition to the behaviors of war or violence as a means of settling disputes or of gaining an advantage. Pacifism covers a spectrum of views ranging from the belief that international disputes can and should all be resolved via peaceful behaviors; to calls for the abolition of various organizations which tend to institutionalize aggressive behaviors, such as the military, or arms manufacturers; to opposition to any organization of society that might rely in any way upon governmental force. Such groups which sometimes oppose the governmental use of force include anarchists and

libertarians. Absolute pacifism opposes violent behavior under all circumstances, including the defense of self and others.

Pacifism may be based on moral principles (a deontological view) or pragmatism (a consequentialist view). Principled pacifism holds that all forms of violent behavior are inappropriate responses to conflict, and are morally wrong. Pragmatic pacifism holds that the costs of war and interpersonal violence are so substantial that better ways of resolving disputes must be found.

Psychological or inner peace (i.e. peace of mind) refers to a state of being internally or spiritually at peace, with sufficient knowledge and understanding to keep oneself calm in the face of apparent discord or stress. Being internally "at peace" is considered by many to be a healthy mental state or homeostasis, and to be the opposite of feeling stressed, mentally anxious, or emotionally unstable. Within meditative traditions, the psychological or inward achievement of "peace of mind" is often associated with bliss and happiness.

Peace of mind, serenity, and calmness are descriptions of a disposition free from the effects of stress. In some meditative traditions, inner peace is believed to be a state of consciousness or enlightenment that may be cultivated by various types of meditation, prayer, t'ai chi ch'uan (太极拳, tàijíquán), yoga, or other various types of mental or physical disciplines. Many such practices refer to this peace as an experience of knowing oneself. An emphasis on finding one's inner peace is often associated with traditions such as Buddhism, Hinduism, and some traditional Christian contemplative practices such as monasticism, as well as with the New Age movement.

The Non-Aggression Principle (NAP) asserts that aggression against an individual or an individual's property is always an immoral violation of one's life, liberty, and property rights. Utilizing deceit instead of consent to achieve ends is also a violation of the Non-Aggression principle. Therefore, under the framework of the Non-Aggression principle, rape, murder, deception, involuntary taxation, government regulation, and other behaviors that initiate aggression against otherwise peaceful individuals are considered violations of this principle. This principle is most commonly adhered to by libertarians. A common elevator pitch for this principle is, "Good ideas don't require force.

Satyagraha is a philosophy and practice of nonviolent resistance developed by Mohandas Karamchand Gandhi. He deployed satyagraha techniques in campaigns for Indian independence and also during his earlier struggles in South Africa.

The word satyagraha itself was coined through a public contest that Gandhi sponsored through the newspaper he published in South Africa, Indian

Opinion when he realized that neither the common, contemporary Hindu language nor the English language contained a word that fully expressed his own meanings and intentions when he talked about his nonviolent approaches to conflict. According to Gandhi's autobiography, the contest winner was Maganlal Gandhi (presumably no relation), who submitted the entry 'satyagraha', which Gandhi then modified to 'satyagraha'. Etymologically, this Hindic word means 'truth-firmness', and is commonly translated as 'steadfastness in the truth' or 'truth-force'.

Satyagraha's theory also influenced Martin Luther King Jr., James Bevel, and others during the campaigns they led during the civil rights movement in the United States. The theory of satyagraha sees means and ends as inseparable. Therefore, it is contradictory to try to use violence to obtain peace. As Gandhi wrote: "They say, 'means are, after all, means'. I would say, 'means are, after all, everything'. As the means so the end..."This a quote sometimes attributed to Gandhi, but also to A. J. Muste sums it up: "There is no way to peace; peace is the way".

Peace-building is a post-Cold War concept and practice. Peace building is a complex and multidimensional exercise that encompasses tasks ranging from the disarming of warring factions to the rebuilding of political, economic, judicial and civil society institutions. It utilizes a variety of actors, ideally, in the construction of a culture of peace to replace a structure of violence. Ever since Johan

Galtung coined the term 'peace building' back in the 1970s, there have been very few attempts to flesh out the essence of this concept. It is only recently, beginning with Boutros Boutros-Ghali's use of the term in his An Agenda for Peace, in which he defined it broadly as 'action to identify and support structures which tend to strengthen and solidify peace to avoid a relapse into conflict'. The introduction of peace-building as a legitimate area for UN attention reflected postCold War optimism about the potential for international collective action to resolve violent conflict among and within states. There was an emerging consensus that conflict, particularly the intra-state conflicts dominating the 1990s, was inextricably linked with underdevelopment and inequality. This facilitated increased UN engagement in the management of peace. Peace-building went beyond physical security and reconstruction. It involved non-military instruments and addressed the political, social and economic development of a post-conflict society. There has been an increase in complex UN peace operations in the 1990s — involving significant civilian as well as military components. The reasons also included with mandates that required disarmament, human rights, election monitoring, refugee return and support for the rebuilding of state institutions. The difficulty of a linear progression from peacemaking, via peacekeeping to peace-building was clear. Many of the conflicts in which the UN and other international actors were engaged throughout the 1990s proved resistant to such an orderly sequence. Relapse into armed conflict, sporadic political violence and public disorder were persistent challenges for peace operations deploying to civil conflicts. These challenges led to increased emphasis on the need for an earlier start to peace-building activities to provide incentives to commit to peace as well as to build confidence in its potential durability among post-conflict populations. In this unit, you will read about these. Aims and Objectives After going through this Unit, you will be able to : ? know the importance of peace building; ? know the challenges facing peace building processes; ? understand the problem of managing balance between short and long term objectives; and ? the ways to tackle the challenges. 4.2 PEACE BUILDING CHALLENGES: HISTORIC OVERVIEW The end of the Cold War changed the nature of the threats to peace and security and called for a re-examination of methodologies for dealing with violent conflicts. The breakdown of the East/ West dynamic changed the basis for state interaction and several long-standing conflicts such as Cambodia, Afghanistan, Angola, Mozambique and El Salvador that came to an end, although each for reasons of its own. However, in the immediate post-Cold War period of the mid nineties, conflicts in Somalia, Rwanda and Haiti were stark reminders that the end of the Cold War did not usher in an era of peace and stability, but the nature of conflicts changed with a number of largely intra-state conflicts finding the space to erupt. As a result, the international community grappled with the challenges of identifying diagnostics, and developing policy instruments and new practices. There were incremental efforts to overcome the shortcomings of existing tools and approaches, and encourage more integrated efforts of a range of actors who had traditionally worked in their own sectors – whether in peace building, peacekeeping, humanitarian relief or development, with human rights issues gradually playing a more important role. 4.3 THE CHALLENGES Peace building is a dynamic process. The features of this process and dynamics of how they unfold and interact at country level are different and depend to a great extent on the Challenges of Peace-Building 43 44 Introduction to Peace and Conflict Management specific country context. Even within the same country, perceptions of what is a priority may change according to the region or the actors concerned. This makes decisions on how to best priorities and sequence support to country-level peace building and state building efforts particularly difficult for both national and for international actors. Identifying the most critical risks of instability the most likely drivers of peace can be a useful way to address this challenge, and indeed appear to have guided the peace building and state building strategies. Common challenges in peace building and state building processes and in national and international support to peace building and state building objectives include: the lack of a shared vision for peace and long-term development; the difficult balance between short and long-term objectives; weak strategic planning and priority setting and low implementation rates; inefficient financing practices; poor institutional arrangements; centralised approaches; lack of citizen participation poor strategic communication; weak accountability between national and international partners; and ineffective donor support etc. 4.3.1 Lack of Shared Vision While a coherent national vision for peace building is considered as a priority and a key outcome of political process, in most instances such a vision either does not exist or is not shared within the country or region. The lack of a shared vision for peace and development between national and international partners is the key challenge to the peace building operations. The following factors were identified as limiting the development of a shared vision for peace building: i) the lack of a shared understanding of the context; ii) the absence of an agreed theory of change over the long term; iii) the difficulty of integrating different country realities into one vision; and iv) the tendency to focus on immediate priorities and interventions unsuited to address the multiple dimensions of the peace building challenge. 4.3.2 Challenges to Managing Balance between Short-Term and LongTerm Objectives It is found that there is existence of trade-offs between short-term and long-term peace building objectives, and the difficulty of making choices that risk undermining some aspects of state building while supporting immediate peace building priorities, and vice versa. Difficult choices are made by actors between aligning support to the long-term political settlement versus short-term deals brokered between elite and power-sharing arrangements that secured peace initially. The result is a decision to support compromised and inefficient governance. Tensions also emerged from the impetus to deliver services quickly to meet urgent needs and maintain stability, and longer-term objectives to build state capacity. It is found that there are mixed views on the concept of "buying peace" (i.e. government provision of cash transfers to help internally displaced people reintegrate into the community following the crisis). While there was general agreement that this was a successful short-term intervention and a likely long-term investment in peace, actors also highlighted the importance of respect for inclusion in order to build lasting peace. 4.4 STRATEGIES, PLANNING AND PRIORITY SETTING The lack of a shared vision for change and the difficult choices that need to be made between short and long-term objectives impact on the strength of strategic planning processes and on the identification and articulation of specific peace building and state building objectives and priorities. Common problems highlighted include the following. 4.4.1 Proliferation of Plans and Strategic Frameworks The existence of several planning documents often developed at the request of donors, and the absence of one single strategic framework that addresses and prioritizes peace building objectives often result in what is described as "disjointed incrementalism". The fragmentation of donor-funded activities, which occurs and persists to a great extent because of the absence of government leadership and because of a continued tendency of donors to seek to implement their own programmes, is both a cause and a symptom of this challenge. This is further complicated by the fact that different donors have different plans and strategies guiding their funding and implementation decisions – e.g. the UN has its UNDAF; the World Bank has its Country Assistance Strategy; and bilateral donors have different types of strategy plans. 4.4.2 Challenges to Operational Alignment There are difficulties associated with the transition between various phases of assistance (e.g. humanitarian, peace building and state building, development), and the inherent tradeoff between being flexible enough to adapt to quick changes on the ground and identifying and aligning with sub-national priorities and plans. It is also noted that international actors have found it difficult to quickly adapt their plans and strategies, to shift gears between longer-term development and emergency response, and to fully align their programmes on national priorities and systems in an environment where national plans and priorities have been annually adjusted to meet what have often been rapidly changing contexts. 4.4.3 Low Rates of Implementation The low rate of implementation of national strategic plans, even when good plans are in place, is identified as a major challenge in peace building operations. Weak managerial and leadership capacity or commitment, and/or the lack of realistic assessment of capacity and of politics – in particular by donors – are seen as some of the causes for poor performance in this area. The lack of consensus on what constitutes "successful implementation" and the absence of conflict-sensitive approaches to the design of policies and programmers are identified as challenges to the peace building and state building process. Lack of prioritization, unrealistic timelines, weak government absorptive capacity at central and local level, inappropriate funding mechanisms and lack of co-ordination within the government and with international partners are all identified as causes of poor progress with implementation of peace building plans. 4.5 FINANCING PRACTICES Poor and inefficient donor financing practices are identified as a fundamental challenge to peace building. Common problems appear to be: i) the short-term horizon and the lack of flexibility of donor funding; Challenges of Peace-Building 45 46 Introduction to Peace and Conflict Management ii) the weak alignment of funding to nationally owned planning processes and priorities; and iii) specific aid modalities. These practices may affect state legitimacy, capacity and responsiveness, as funds cannot be committed to long-

term reforms critical for state building; sectors vital to peace building. State building remains underfunded; and the way funds are delivered may not respond to the needs and expectations of national partners. It is also found that aid allocations in many cases do not correspond to the identified need. Lack of data on country-wide poverty levels and aid volatility make it difficult for the government to sustain service delivery, which can easily contribute to undermining citizens' trust. 4.6 STRUCTURAL CHALLENGES The peace builders, both intra-state and inter-state, face many structural challenges in their efforts to bring and consolidate peace. Following are important in that: 4.6.1 Institutional Arrangements Weak institutional arrangements within and between national government departments affect the strategic planning processes and implementation, which may lead to compartmentalised approaches to addressing peace building challenges. The donor practice of dealing with single institutions (e.g. ministries) on a bilateral basis, instead of supporting cross-departmental capacities, contributes to this problem. The proliferation of institutional structures, also promoted by donors, is another factor affecting the building of state capacity. The lack of clarity on roles and responsibilities among government actors and the donor practice of engaging with individual ministries are also reasons for the weak implementation of agreed priorities and for disjointed interventions. Weak institutional arrangements between government agencies are a major impediment to effective peace building. 4.6.2 Executive and Capital-Centric Approaches The focus of national and international attention on the capital and on a few central state actors (e.g. the executive) was generally seen as characteristic of, yet challenging to, peace building and state building. The risks of rural-urban divide in aid and too narrow a focus on central institutions and on the executive are considered as contributing to the creation of "islands of capability" within a generally dysfunctional system, leaving aside more inclusive approaches to development and seriously affecting overall state capacities and legitimacy. It is also found that the over-centralisation of development, politics and services has exacerbated regional frictions, because district administrations in rural areas, where the majority of the population lives, remain weak and service delivery low. There is also a risk of developing central government capacities beyond sustainable means. These issues can become particularly damaging where international actors fail to analyse the nature of the social contract, or grasp the complexity and fragility of a political settlement in a country. 4.6.3 Citizen Participation Enhancing citizens' participation and ensuring that they gain ownership of government policy formulation and implementation are considered as important components of a renewed governance system and of the social contract underpinning it. However, effective involvements of civil society in key decision-making and planning contexts are rare. Civil society, community-based organisations and ordinary citizens are not fully involved in peace building programmes, which created a situation where the government is seen as going it alone. Ensuring citizens' participation at all stages of the design and implementation of interventions in support of peace building and broader development objectives are seen as a challenging yet key area for long-term stability. There is need for civil society participation, to enable the government to understand and respond to people's expectations and consequently to rebuild the trust between the state and citizens. However, Statecentric and capital-centric approaches to peace building promoted by national and international partners do not help create space for civil society actors. 4.6.4 Poor Strategic Communication The lack of communication is identified as a real challenge to the advancement of the peace building and state building agenda. Unsurprisingly, strategic communication in fragile and conflict-affected countries is seldom a priority, despite being a critical element for change and for efforts to increase the legitimacy and accountability of the state. Communicating government decisions in regard to critical peace building goals and interventions contributes to aligning interest and getting support for difficult reforms. The lack of strategic communications from the centre, associated with the weaknesses of a leadership is a major factor affecting the consolidation and advancement of the peace building process. 4.6.5 Limited Accountability of International Partners While mutual accountability features highly in the aid effectiveness agenda, poor accountability on the donor side has been a key feature of the relationship between national and international partners engaged in fragile and conflict-affected contexts. This concern is becoming even more important as donors become increasingly engaged in supporting highly complex peace building processes. Even when mutual accountability is an objective of a peace building framework for collaboration between national and international partners, often the actual commitments of international actors are not spelled out clearly enough, and efforts to review actions against international commitments have been weak. 4.6.6 Limited Effectiveness of Capacity Development Approaches Donor approaches to capacity development continue to be piecemeal, and they fail to address cross-government and systemic challenges. Reliance on foreign technical assistance and the poor rate of transfer of skills and knowledge are found to undermine the capacity, accountability, and legitimacy of the state in the eyes of citizens. Weak transfer of skills and technical capacity, quick turnover of "advisers", significant levels of "brain-drain" (government officials leaving their jobs to work for donor agencies), and the lack of coherent, long-term capacity development programmers are seen as affecting significant progress in this area. Related to the problem of ineffective donor support to capacity development is the use of parallel systems. The reluctance of donors to take risks and to use country systems for implementing donor-supported activities often leads to the use and multiplication of parallel project implementation units. One of the reasons for such units is the difficulty faced by partner countries in putting in place adequate management and reporting systems. Challenges of Peace-Building 47 48 Introduction to Peace and Conflict Management 4.6.7 Legitimacy Challenges The issue of legitimacy is serious, although less frequently addressed, challenge for peace-building. Contemporary peace-building as state-building is founded on the assumption that a particular type of state can best guarantee human rights and development, that is, one founded on democratic principles. In today's globalized world, the democratic state has taken on a particular paradigm—the liberal market economy state. Large parts of the Industrialised world hold this paradigm to be the most efficient and sustainable model for democratic statehood and the model for developing countries. Thus, peace-building not only involves external actors in the internal workings of the state but also prescribes the direction of that transformation. This is a highly political endeavor that raises important questions of legitimacy at the international and local levels. 4.7 SUMMARY This unit highlighted a series of challenges and bottlenecks that impede the peace-building processes. These include lack of a shared vision for change among key stakeholders for peace and long-term development; lack of context and conflict analysis, the difficult balance between short and long-term objectives; lack of trust between developing countries and development partners; too many overlapping plans, and weak alignment of donors behind a unified national plan; lack of agreement on the need to address shifting short-term and long-term priorities at the same time; weak strategic planning and priority setting and poor implementation rates; financing practices; poor institutional arrangements; centralised approaches; lack of citizen participation, poor strategic communication; weak accountability between national and international partners; and limited effectiveness of capacity development approaches; insufficient attention to the protection of women and children from armed conflict and to the participation of women in peace building and state building; insufficient attention to economic growth and job creation, particularly for youth etc. These challenges will need to be addressed to promote peace and security and to support capable and legitimate states that can take the lead in national development.

The open debate intends to focus on the various challenges faced by countries in fragile contexts, in particular on the African continent. The discussion is likely to examine the drivers that contribute to creating fragile contexts, their effects, and the role of the Security Council in addressing them.

In Africa, multiple factors contribute to creating fragile contexts, including insecurity, intercommunal violence, organised crime, terrorism, violent extremism, socio-economic inequality, weak governance, youth marginalisation, the illegal exploitation of natural resources, competition for scarce resources, and climate change. These drivers also have the potential to contribute to armed conflict and exacerbate threats to international peace and security.

The Council mandates several UN missions in African countries facing these complex challenges, including the UN Multidimensional Integrated Stabilization Mission in Mali (MINUSMA); the UN Organization Stabilization Mission in the Democratic Republic of the Congo (MONUSCO); the UN Multidimensional Integrated Stabilization Mission in the Central African Republic (MINUSCA); the UN Mission in South Sudan (UNMISS) and the UN Assistance Mission in Somalia (UNSOM).

The impact of the COVID-19 pandemic, declared a global health crisis on 11 March 2020 by the World

Health Organization, is also relevant in this context. Resolution 2532, adopted on 1 July 2020 following an arduous negotiation, demanded an immediate cessation of hostilities in all situations on the Council's agenda in support of the Secretary-General's global ceasefire appeal to combat the pandemic. The resolution also recognised the risks to fragile states that have been affected by conflict, cautioning that peacebuilding and development gains made by countries in transition and in post-conflict situations could be reversed as a result of the pandemic. On 9 September 2020, Security Council members held an open videoconference (VTC) on the implementation of resolution 2532. Under-Secretary-General for Humanitarian Affairs Mark Lowcock said the weakest, most fragile and conflict-affected countries would be those worst affected by COVID-19 in the medium and long term. Under-Secretary-General for Political and Peacebuilding Affairs Rosemary DiCarlo said the erosion of trust in public institutions "increases fragility and has the potential to drive instability".

The Council has engaged on several of the factors that contribute to fragile contexts in both thematic and country-specific items on its agenda. As a recent example, Security Council members held a virtual, high-level open debate on 3 November 2020 on "contemporary drivers of conflict and insecurity", under the Peacebuilding and Sustaining Peace agenda at the initiative of Saint Vincent and the Grenadines, which looked at the security implications of climate change and COVID-19, among other factors.

Council Dynamics

Some Council members hold conservative views of what constitutes a threat to peace and security. These members are likely to be more reluctant for the Council to engage on certain issues, including in relation to climate change and some socio-economic factors. Russia and China have expressed concern that Council involvement on such issues encroaches on the prerogatives of other UN entities, which they maintain are better equipped to deal with them. Russia has been the most notably vocal and often cautions about the value of maintaining the division of labour between the UN's principal organs and its peace and security, development and human rights pillars.

The security implications of climate change is a particularly controversial issue in the Council. Most Council members currently champion the organ's engagement on this issue. They have emphasised that factors such as drought, water scarcity, food insecurity, and desertification that are caused or exacerbated by climate change increase the risk of violent conflict. Russia, China and the US, however, have strong reservations about the Council's engagement on this issue. The US has resisted efforts to incorporate climate-security language in Council outcomes on Iraq, Haiti and other matters.

After initial concerns raised by China and South Africa about the COVID-19 pandemic's link with the maintenance of peace and security, members appear to recognise and agree on its potential peace and security implications.

CHAPTER FOUR

Theories

Many different theories of "peace" exist in the world of peace studies, which involves the study of de-escalation, conflict transformation, disarmament, and cessation of violence. The definition of "peace" can vary with religion, culture, or subject of study.

Balance of power

The classical "realist" position is that the key to promoting order between states, and so of increasing the chances of peace, is the maintenance of a balance of power between states – a situation where no state is so dominant that it can "lay down the law to the rest". Exponents of this view have included Metternich, Bismarck, Hans Morgenthau, and Henry Kissinger. A related approach – more in the tradition of Hugo Grotius than Thomas Hobbes – was articulated by the so-called "English school of international relations theory" such as Martin Wight in his book Power Politics (1946, 1978) and Hedley Bull in The Anarchical Society (1977).

As the maintenance of a balance of power could in some circumstances require a willingness to go to war, some critics saw the idea of a balance of power as promoting war rather than promoting peace. This was a radical critique of those supporters of the Allied and Associated Powers who justified entry into World War I on the grounds that it was necessary to preserve the balance of power in Europe from a German bid for hegemony.

In the second half of the 20th century, and especially during the cold war, a particular form of balance of power – mutual nuclear deterrence – emerged as a widely held doctrine on the key to peace between the great powers. Critics argued that the development of nuclear stockpiles increased the chances of war rather than peace, and that the "nuclear umbrella" made it "safe" for smaller wars (e.g. the Vietnam war and the Soviet invasion of Czechoslovakia to end the Prague Spring), so making such wars more likely.

Free trade and interdependence

It was a central tenet of classical liberalism, for example among English liberal thinkers of the late 19th and early 20th century, that free trade promoted peace. For example, the Cambridge economist John Maynard Keynes (1883–1946) said that he was "brought up" on this idea and held it unquestioned until at least the 1920s. During the economic globalization in the decades leading up to World War I, writers such as Norman Angell argued that the growth of economic interdependence between the great powers made war between them futile and therefore unlikely. He made this argument in 1913. A year later Europe's economically interconnected states were embroiled in what would later become known as the First World War.

Democratic peace theory

The democratic peace theory posits that democracy causes peace because of the accountability, institutions, values, and norms of democratic countries.

Territorial peace theory

The territorial peace theory posits that peace causes democracy because territorial wars between neighbor countries lead to authoritarian attitudes and disregard for democratic values. This theory is supported by historical studies showing that countries rarely become democratic until after their borders have been settled by territorial peace with neighboring countries.

War game

The Peace and War Game is an approach in game theory to understand the relationship between peace and conflicts.

The iterated game hypotheses were originally used by academic groups and computer simulations to study possible strategies of cooperation and aggression.

As peacemakers became richer over time, it became clear that making war had greater costs than initially anticipated. One of the well-studied strategies that acquired wealth more rapidly was based on Genghis Khan, i.e. a constant aggressor making war continually to gain resources. This led, in contrast, to the development of what's known as the "provokable nice guy strategy", a peace-maker until attacked, improved upon merely to win by occasional forgiveness even when attacked. By adding the results of all pairwise games for each player, one sees that multiple players gain wealth cooperating with each other while bleeding a constantly aggressive player.

Socialism and managed capitalism

Socialist, communist, and left-wing liberal writers of the 19th and 20th centuries (e.g., Lenin, J.A. Hobson, John Strachey) argued that capitalism caused war (e.g. through promoting imperial or other economic rivalries that lead to international conflict). This led some to argue that international socialism was the key to peace.

However, in response to such writers in the 1930s who argued that capitalism caused the war, the economist John Maynard Keynes (1883–1946) argued that managed capitalism could promote peace. This involved international coordination of fiscal/ monetary policies, an international monetary system that did not pit the interests of countries against each other, and a high degree of freedom of trade. These ideas underlay Keynes's work during World War II that led to the creation of the International Monetary Fund and the World Bank at Bretton Woods in 1944, and later of the General Agreement on Tariffs and Trade (subsequently the World Trade Organization).

International organization and law

One of the most influential theories of peace, especially since Woodrow Wilson led the creation of the League of Nations at the Paris Peace Conference of 1919, is that peace will be advanced if the intentional anarchy of states is replaced through the growth of international law promoted and enforced through international organizations such as the League of Nations, the United Nations, and other functional international organizations. One of the most important early exponents of this view was Alfred Eckhart Zimmern, for example in his 1936 book The League of Nations and the Rule of Law.

Trans-national solidarity

Many "idealist" thinkers about international relations – e.g. in the traditions of Kant and Karl Marx – have argued that the key to peace is the growth of some form of solidarity between peoples (or classes of people) spanning the lines of cleavage between nations or states that lead to war.

One version of this is the idea of promoting international understanding between nations through the international mobility of students – an idea most

powerfully advanced by Cecil Rhodes in the creation of the Rhodes Scholarships, and his successors such as J. William Fulbright.

• 53 •

Another theory is that peace can be developed among countries on the basis of active management of water resources.

CHAPTER FIVE

Challenges

The range of potential threats to peace and security addressed by the panel are likely to be grouped under six broad headings:

threats from poverty, disease, and environmental breakdown (the threats to human security identified in the Millennium Development Goals)

- *threats from conflict between states*

- *threats from violence and massive human rights violations within states*

- *threats from terrorism*

- *threats from organized crime*

- *threats from the proliferation of weapons - particularly WMD, but also conventional*

"While the panel will address the whole range of international players, it nonetheless will have to address a number of institutional problems evident in the UN system, including the perceived unrepresentative structure of the Security Council, the cumbrous and dysfunctional character of much of the economic and social machinery, and the limited role and impact of the general assembly," Evans said.

"The range of the threats facing the world are so urgent and widespread that the United States would prefer to engage multilaterally," said Stewart Patrick of the U.S. State Department Policy Planning Staff. Giving his personal views, Patrick noted that the United Nations is not one entity, but several

organizations including the general assembly, secretariat, secretary-general, and numerous agencies. Thus any reform recommendations must be multi-faceted and encompassing. For instance, he cited the lack of standards and criteria for countries with dubious human rights records, such as Sudan and Libya, and their election to membership and leadership positions in the United Nations Commission on Human Rights.

"The panel is not focusing on reform in a narrow sense," said Abiodun Williams, Head of Strategic Planning, Executive Office of the United Nations Secretary-General. "These changes will be a means to the end, hopefully resulting in a more comprehensive collective security system. "

The Impact of Iraq on the UN

"The military invasion of Iraq may actually be considered a success for the United Nations," said Thomas Leney, Director of Programs, UN Foundation. Before taking action to forcefully remove Saddam Hussein from power, President Bush and his administration attempted to get a United Nations Security Council resolution, and their effort shows the relevance of the United Nations. Still there exists a

great tension between the norms of sovereignty and humanitarian intervention and questions regarding the use of force—especially against the backdrop of Iraq and the Darfur region of Sudan. "This is the needle that we will need to thread, and is the biggest challenge for the panel and the United Nations," Leney said.

The discussion also focused on responses to genocide, the International Criminal Court, and institutional reform. "The challenge of the high-level panel is to make the United Nations work so well that the United States won't be tempted as often to go it alone," Evans said. However, he noted that the invasion of Iraq has made it more difficult to enforce collective security responses to legitimate security concerns.

"Lasting peace and security should be underpinned by adhering to the rule of law," Leney said. Furthermore, he advised moving away from the strict criteria outlined by the genocide convention, instead focusing on the victims of injustice, atrocities, and mass killings. He urged the United States' engagement with the United Nations as it attempts to reshape global norms.

Reconstitution of the Security Council

"Although disproportionate attention has focused on reform of the Security Council, changing its composition and structure to better reflect the reality of the 21ˢᵗ century is indeed a priority," Evans said. The panel is discussing a proposal that would expand the Security Council, with the eventual addition of approximately nine members. New members would be divided into four-year renewable terms and two-year terms as at present, with some allocation of those seats to a revised set of regional groupings. "The system would be formulated in such a way that would make it possible for the major aspirants for permanent membership on the Security Council to play a much more regular role," noted Evans.

Many of the participants agreed with Annan's comments of a year ago—we have reached a fork in the road and more critically, if member states won't make a decision or prefer to keep the status quo, then history will make the decision for all of us.

Waging peace is the greatest issue facing the international community – a question of life and death, of survival or extinction. Such an issue demands thorough reflection and analysis (Sawyer,

1994). Today, peacebuilding is spurred by the awareness that there are limits to violence. We can forget sustainable development if no serious efforts are undertaken for preventing violence and building sustainable peace. Since the end of the Second World War, many scholars have been engaged in the study of war and peace. In the post-Cold War era, there has been an increasing demand for peace research, and its findings are now being used by decision-makers and practitioners. The European Union (EU), one of the leading international bodies to affirm the importance of peace-building and conflict prevention, is building up its capacity for these activities (Moyroud, Lund, and Mehler, 1999). The same is true for the United 2 Challenges of Peace Research Nations (UN). The Report of the High-level Panel on Threats, Challenges, and Change offers new ideas for improving the UN's performance, including the creation of a new inter-governmental body, the 'Peacebuilding Commission', whose task would be to assist states that are under stress or recovering from conflict in the development of their capacity to perform their sovereign functions effectively and responsibly (United Nations, 2004). Various ministries or departments in many countries have established conflict prevention units. Intervention projects, programs, and policies are subjected to proactive peace and conflict impact assessments (PCIAS). PCIAS is a process of determining the relevance of ongoing or proposed interventions and predicting their future effects on the conflict dynamics and peace-building process. This assessment is system-oriented and proactive. It is intended to increase both the conflict sensitivity and the peace benefits of the intervention. Governmental and non-governmental organizations dealing with a broad range of peace-building activities are mushrooming. In their global survey of armed conflicts, Robert Gurr et al. (2001) depict the world as more peaceful than at any time in the past century. The number and magnitude of armed conflicts within and among states have lessened since the 1990s by nearly half. Conflicts over self-determination are being settled with ever greater frequency, usually when ethnic groups gain greater autonomy and power-sharing within existing states (Gurr, Marshall, and Khosla, 2003). The progress is attributed to the increase in conflict prevention efforts and the greater number of democratic efforts. This is the good news. But now let us take a look at three other, more sobering observations. Three Sobering Observations 1. High Levels of Manifest and Potential Violence In contrast to these statistics, the overall level of manifest and latent violence is still high. Most databanks on conflicts monitor the most visible types of violence. A different picture appears when a broader definition of violence is used, namely: (a) when violence is defined as a situation in which the quantitative and qualitative life expectancies (measured, for instance, through the Human Security Index) of a particular group or groups within a community, a state, a region or the world are significantly lower than other groups, and (b) when this can be attributed to one or more sources of violence: physical violence, structural violence, psychological violence, cultural violence, bad governance, organized crime or extra-legal activities (Reychler and Jacobs, 2004). The difference between armed violence and other types of violence is that armed violence is direct and visible, and it kills faster.

The other types of violence are indirect and less visible, and they affect more people. Gandhi (n.d.) called poverty the worst form of violence: "Earth provides enough to satisfy every man's need, but not every man's greed". It affects a billion people who live on $1 a day, and 2.8 billion who live on less Luc Reychler 3 than $2 a day. In the West poverty means living a bad life; in the Third World, it means surviving in a state close to death (Zakaria, 2005). Mapping the whole fabric of violence, including its less visible forms, gives a more realistic picture of violence in the contemporary world. Paradoxically, the media and researchers continue to focus on sensational violence (terrorism, irregular and conventional warfare), which kills less than the other forms of violence. Terrorism causes approximately 5,000 deaths a year, and anti-terrorism and conventional warfare cause a hundred times this number (500,000), but structural violence shortens the life span of hundreds of millions of people, and bad governance reduces the life expectations of approximately 1.5 billion people. Calling terrorism the greatest threat in the world masks most of the violence in today's world. Bad governance has many faces. It can express itself as: (a) greed and corruption: infant mortality increases by 75% when the level of corruption increases from medium to a high level; (b) indifference and neglect: think of the ongoing genocidal conflicts in Chechnya and Sudan; (c) ignorance and stupidity: remember Mao's Great Leap Forward in China, which caused the death of millions of Chinese, or the retreat of the Blue Helmets from Rwanda in 1994 when the genocidal violence started; or (d) the harmful and negative side-effects of well-intentioned policies (Reychler and Jacobs,

2004). *Bad governance kills. Another source of violence is the activities of transnational organized crime. It is estimated that criminal organizations earn $300 to $500 billion annually from narcotics trafficking, their single largest source of income. The last strand in the fabric of violence is the "shadows of war". Carolyn Nordstrom (2004) describes this as the complex sets of cross-state economic and political linkages that move outside recognized state-based channels and in many cases have greater power than some of the world's states. This set of economic and personnel flows ranges from the mundane (the trade in cigarettes and pirated software), through the elicit (gems and timber), to the dangerous (weapons and illegal narcotics). Initial inquiries estimate the amount of money generated per year through extra-state activities to be in trillions of euros (Nordstrom, 2004). These amounts dwarf the budgets of international organizations such as the EU and the UN. The EU's budget in 2004 was €99.52 billion; the budget of the UN for 2002-2003 was $2.6 billion. Part of this money could be used to support the Millennium Development Goals (MDGs), which require $135 million in 2006 and $195 million in 2015. These are huge opportunity losses for conflict prevention and peacebuilding. To prevent violence more effectively, one has to look at the whole fabric of violence. Armed violence is intertwined with the other strands of the fabric. Before the genocide erupted in Rwanda with volcanic force, the country was considered a relatively secure place. A broader analysis of the violence would have warned us better about the growing tensions in the country (Uvin, 1998). The price of a narrow analysis of violence is a surprise. n. Spokespersons from Third World* *countries decry the structural violence and unfair intervention in the international environment (Reychler, 1979). The resilience of this gap causes discomfort, dissatisfaction and frustration among peace researchers. Some researchers have become cynical: they find it difficult to live with the wide gap and assert that all the research is a waste of time; it produces theories, but no results. Some are burned out and have stopped contributing to the field. Others continue to look at the bright side of life and stick to the 'law of the hammer' (If my only tool is a hammer, everything becomes a nail.) They are convinced that more of the same will lead to peace. Most peace researchers, however, have turned the tension into a creative re-search for more cost-effective ways to build sustainable peace. Peace research requires strongly motivated people because: (1) It is a demanding field of study. (2) Peace still has image problems; it can evoke either hope and strength or despair and weakness. (3) Compared to the traditional fields of study, peace research is academically less embedded; it transcends the barriers of faculties and departments. (4) It deals with 'senti-mental' walls. Senti-mental walls are the theories, assumptions, expectations, attitudes, feelings, taboos, beliefs, norms and principles that stand in the way of conflict prevention and peace building. It is important to identify and dismantle them. Frequently, this goes hand in hand with emotional and other kinds of resistance. Cynicism or defeatism can inhibit the peace building process seriously. (5) Transforming violent conflicts can be exhausting. Four challenges can be distinguished. Challenges of Peace Research If peace researchers want to make a greater difference, they have to challenge the ways and means of the current practice of peace making, peace-keeping and peacebuilding. Challenge 1: Seeing the Big Picture The first challenge is not to lose sight of the big picture. Peace building is the result of the activities of many people in different sectors and at different levels. These skills are acquired through education and practice. Effective peace building also implies that the peace builders see where and how their efforts fit into the peace building process. Seeing the big picture is vital for coherent peace building efforts. The big picture or macro-perspective gives an overview of the necessary peace building blocks. It enables the peace builders to oversee and coordinate what they are doing. The essential requirements or preconditions for creating sustainable peace – which have been derived from the peace research – can be clustered into five peace building blocks: (1) an effective system of communication, consultation and negotiation; (2) 6 Challenges of Peace Research peace-enhancing structures and institutions; (3) an integrative political-psychological climate; (4) a critical mass of peace building leadership; and (5) a supportive international environment. These peace building blocks are all necessary and mutually reinforcing. The deficiency or absence of one of these building blocks can seriously undermine the stability or effectiveness of the entire peace building process. In addition to these five clusters, there are the necessary support systems (legal, educational, health, humanitarian aid, information and environment al systems) that play an important role in the peace building process. The first building block focuses on the establishment of an effective communication, consultation and negotiation system at different levels between the conflicting parties or members. In contrast to the negotiation styles used in most international organizations, the negotiation style in the European Union is predominantly integrative. Ample time and creativity is invested in generating mutually benefiting agreements. Without win-win agreements, the Union would disintegrate. The second building block consists of peace-enhancing structures. In order to achieve a sustainable peace, (conflict) countries have to install political, economic and security structures and institutions that sustain peace. The political reform process aims at the establishment of political structures with a high level of legitimacy. The legitimacy status is influenced by two factors: (a) the ability of a regime to deliver vital basic needs, such as security, health services, jobs, and so forth; and (b) the democratic procedure. Initially, an authoritarian regime with high quality leaders and technocrats can get a high legitimacy score, but in the end, consolidated democracies provide the best support for sustainable peace building. It is crucial to note that the transition from one state (e.g. nondemocratic structures) to another (e.g. consolidated democratic environment) is not without difficulties: the devil is in the transition (Reychler, 1999). The economic reform process envisions the establishment of an economic environment which stimulates sustainable development and the reduction of gross vertical and horizontal inequalities. The security structures safeguard and/or increase the population's objective and subjective security by effectively dealing with both internal and external threats. This implies a cooperative security system producing a high level of human security, collective defense and security, and proactive conflict prevention efforts. In addition to these 'three core peace building structures', there is also a need to build effective judicial, educational, health and environmental systems to sustain the peace building process. As long as these structures are not in place, humanitarian aid will be needed. The third necessary building block for establishing a sustainable peace process is an integrative climate (Reychler and Langer, 2003). This is the software of peace building. This building block stresses the importance of a favorable social-psychological environment. Although the climate is less tangible and observable than the other building blocks, it can be assessed by looking at the consequences. An integrative or disintegrative climate can express itself in the form of attitudes, behavior and institutions. The characteristics of an integrative climate include: expectations of an attractive future as a Luc Reychler 7 consequence of cooperation; the development of a sense of 'we -ness', multiple loyalties, reconciliation, trust and social capital; and the dismantlement of senti-mental walls.*

The fourth building block is a supportive regional and international environment. The stability of a peace process is often dependent on the behavior and interests of neighboring countries or regional powers. These actors can have a positive influence on the peace process by providing political legitimacy or support, by assisting with the demobilization and demilitarization process, and by facilitating and stimulating regional trade and economic integration. However, these same actors can also inhibit the progress towards stability, for example, by supporting certain groups that do not subscribe to the peace process. Likewise, the larger international community plays a crucial role in most post-conflict countries. Via UN agencies or other international (non-)governmental organizations, the international community can provide crucial resources and funding or even take direct responsibility for a wide variety of tasks, such as the (physical) rebuilding process, political transformation, humanitarian aid, development cooperation, third-party security guarantor, and so forth. Peace enhancing political, economic and security structures. Integrative climate Multilateral Cooperationsupport Critical mass of peace building leadership Effective system communication, consultation and negotiation 8 Challenges of Peace Research The fifth building block is the presence of a critical mass of peace building leadership (Reychler and Stellamans, 2005). There are leaders in different domains (politics, diplomacy, defense, economics, education, media, religion, health, and so forth) and at different levels: the elite, middle and grassroots levels (Lederach, 1997). High on the agenda of architectural research should be research to identify the characteristics of successful peace building leaders, such as Nelson Mandela, F. W. De Klerk, Mohandas Gandhi, Mikhail Gorbachev, Vaclav Havel, Jean Monnet, Helmut Kohl, George Marshal, Martin Luther King, Jacques Delors, and many others. This research involves differentiating successful and unsuccessful peace builders and identifying the similarities and differences between successful and unsuccessful peace builders, and between peace builders and peace destroyers (Reychler and Stellamans, 2002). Peace building leaders distinguish themselves by the way they lead the conflict transformation process. They envision a *shared, clear and mutually attractive peaceful future for all who want to cooperate; they do everything possible to identify and get a full understanding of the challenge with which they are confronted; they frame the conflict in a reflexive way (Rothman, 1997); their change behavior is adaptive , integrative and flexible; they are well acquainted with non-violent methods; they use a mix of intentional and consequential ethics and objectives; and they are courageous men and women with a high level of integrity. Challenge 2: Mastering Sustainable Peace Building Architecture The second challenge is to get a better understanding of the sustainable peace building architecture. Despite a more supportive international environment, the costs and risks associated with peace building remain high. The experiences from Germany to Iraq have shown successes and failures. Winning the war can sometimes be relatively easy – or at least rapid – but, as RAND (2003; 2005) studies underscore, winning the peace that prevents a return to war can be a far more complex and time-consuming enterprise. The price of the regime change in Iraq is turning out to be higher than expected. The costs can be apprehended in terms of human losses (on the allied side approximately 2,000 have died and 20,000 have been wounded; the number of Iraqis killed is estimated at 100,000), financial expenses (the Bush administration has spent $200 billion; this is more than the budget of the World Bank or the EU), material destruction and diplomatic damage. Iraq and other cases make it very clear that we need to learn to build sustainable peace in a more effective, cost-efficient and satisfactory way. This demands a better understanding of the architecture of peace building. The term 'peace building architecture' refers to the* *art and science of successful peace building (Reychler, 2002). Peace architecture studies show how conflicts can be transformed in a more effective, efficient and satisfactory way. This requires coherent planning and a good understanding of the cross-impact of different peace building efforts (diplomatic, political, economic, security, psychological, and others). The aim is to synergize these efforts and reduce possible negative side- Luc Reychler 9 effects. The key variables in architectural research are timing (simultaneous or sequential) and priority setting (Reychler and Langer, 2004). Time makes the difference between life and death. Comparative studies of successful peace building efforts can further our insight into the peace architecture. One of the tools which need further development is the peace and conflict impact assessment methodology (Reychler and Paffenholz, 2004). The aim is to identify the relevance and future consequences of an ongoing or proposed intervention on the conflict dynamics and peace building process. The assessment is system-oriented and proactive. It is meant to increase the conflictsensitivity and the peace 'added value' of intervention. The peace and conflict impact assessment system could play a useful role at the different levels of intervention (project, program, sector and broad policy levels) by increasing the awareness of the potential or actual impact on the conflict dynamics and peace building process, and by helping to design more coherent interventions which do no harm and have a higher peace added value. This methodology can be used for improving the design and implementation of interventions ranging from development or humanitarian work to peace and reconciliation or democratization efforts taking place in situations of latent or manifest violent conflict - or in the aftermath of a violent conflict or war. The method consists of (1) preparatory steps to inform and commit the organization to the assessment process, (2) a conflict analysis and prognosis, (3) a peace building deficiency assessment, (4) an assessment of the peace relevance, (5) a conflict risks analysis, (6) an assessment of the impact of the intervention on the peace and conflict, and (7) concrete recommendations and follow-up. Challenge 3: Synergizing the Know-how and Learning The third challenge concerns the slow learning process. The learning of violence prevention and peace building can be improved by (a) making use of different forms of scientific inquiry, (b) providing space for trans-disciplinary research, (c) creating structures which support a better exchange of knowledge between the decision-makers, the practitioners in the field and the research community, (d) inviting the actors involved in peace building to reflect critically on their personal or organizational theories of violence prevention and peace building, and (e) making more effective use of local expertise. (a) Making use of different types of inquiry. Peace research should involve not only classical empirical-analytical research (searching for the causal explanations) and interpretative research (investigating how people perceive their experiences), but also participatory peace action research. The latter type of research is based on the principle that people - ordinary men and women - have a universal right to participate in the production of knowledge that affects their life. Susan Smith (Smith, Willms and Johnson, 1997) calls this "liberatory inquiry". People are not the passive subjects of research, but rather active subjects. Their needs should be the point of departure for knowledge 10 Challenges of Peace Research production and justification of the research (Smith et al., 1997). The initiative of the mothers of soldiers from St. Petersburg to meet the Chechen rebels is a very good example of participatory peace action inquiry. They transcended their passive role as victims and assumed responsibility to transform the conflict and make an end to that ugly war. (b) Provide trans-disciplinary research capacity. If the universities want to play a peace building role, they will have to overcome their preference for uni-disciplinary studies or faculties. Peace building involves changes in complex dynamic systems which can only be understood in a trans-disciplinary way. Progress in peace research means crossing boundaries. In each faculty you have scholars who want to change the world. For the economists, development tends to be seen as the most important factor in the peace building process; for lawyers, it's the rule of law; political scientists point out the importance of democracy; for strategists, security must come first; for psychologists and educators, peace is all about building peace in the minds and hearts of people; theologians stress the importance of mercy, forgiveness and reconciliation; medical doctors stress that a healthy mind resides in a healthy body; and artists believe in the aesthetics of peace building. Most researchers are somewhat narcissistic. Narcissists work with a fervent passion. Their work is their life and their sense of destiny fuels their motivation. They have the ability to work through some of the toughest obstacles (Maccoby and Gschwandtner, 2005). The challenge therefore is not to change, but rather to transform this narrow narcissism into productive narcissism by inviting all to play in the orchestra of peace building. (c) Build structures that support a better exchange of knowledge between the decision-makers, the practitioners in the field and the research community. One of the greatest causes of knowledge waste is the lack of dialogue and the weak connections between the decision-makers and the practitioners in the field (the operari) and the researchers (the speculari). To improve peace building architecture, the development of dialogue and connections between these three sources of knowledge and know-how must be encouraged and rewarded. It is natural that theory and action should be complementary, that they should constitute harmonic aspects of one whole. In reality, however, there exists what has been called a "theory-practice gap" (Lepgold and Nincic, 2002). This gap is caused by the incentive systems of the politicians, of the practitioners in the field and of the researchers (academics). The academic incentive system is characterized by a publish or perish mentality, by the recognition of originality, by the tendency for research methods to triumph over substance, by the preference for fundamental over applied research, by papers filled with jargon, and by the reinforcement of all of this by academic faddishness. The incentive system of the policy makers consists in their need to find timely solutions for concrete problems. Officials have less time to read and reflect. Joseph Nye (Lepgold and Nincic, 2002), one of the few people who have acted both as scholar and as policymaker, was surprised at the "oral" nature of the communication and decision-making culture at the top levels of government service. One Luc Reychler 11 of the major challenges of peace research is to facilitate dialogue and connections between the decision-makers, the practitioners and the research community. Peace researchers have a bridging role: they should not only provide policy-relevant knowledge, but also effectively dialogue with practitioners, especially in instances where the people on each side have interests in common. Peace research can provide instrumental knowledge (e.g. how to prevent groupthink in crisis situations), contextual knowledge (e.g. specifying the necessary conditions for sustainable peace building) and consequential knowledge (e.g. anticipating the costs and consequences of policy options). The most productive exchanges might take place between researchers who have spent some time in government and in the field, and practitioners who have had some academic training in violence prevention and peace building research. All of the above does not imply that the Ivory Tower should be dismantled. It exists for good reasons. It provides the academic freedom without which scientific research is impossible. It also allows the intellectuals to reflect on the world from a certain distance, and not simply to do the work of policy commentators or journalists at a slower pace (Lepgold and Nincic, 2002). (d) Stimulate conscious and competent learning. The learning curve can be raised by stimulating reflective peace research. Policy-makers, practitioners in the field, researchers and educators involved in peace building should reflect on the underlying normative, theoretical and epistemological assumptions of the personal and collective theories or mental models of peace. These mental models, frequently referred to as "common sense", influence the decision-making. Because mental models are usually tacit, existing below the level of awareness, they are often untested and unexamined. They are generally invisible for us, unless we look for them (Senge, 1994). A valuable contribution to reflective peace research has come from Jayne Docherty, who has been developing an interesting and creative approach to reflective peace research. She (Docherty, 2005) distinguishes three types of personal theories: "Baby theories", "Teenage theories", and "Big Grown-up theories". The first are our gut level theories that guide behavior, the second are theories based on practice, and the third are well grounded theories based on systematic research. (e) Make effective use of local expertise. Despite the existence of the 'participatory action research 'rituals, the donors and external interveners in conflicts rely predominantly on the advice of external consultants. The architecture of peace could significantly improve by eliciting local intelligence. Challenge 4: Dealing with the Reality of the Peace Building Context The fourth challenge is to deal effectively with the peace building context, which is characterized by uncertainty, unpredictability, competing values and interests, and the struggle for power. Building peace requires not only analytic skills, but also imagination, creativity, reconciliation of competing values and interests, the implementation of arms and power control, the use of non-violent action, "in extremis" the use of arms, and a 12 Challenges of Peace Research great deal of courage. Hope is not a strategy. Peace researchers can influence the context more favorably by: (a) developing a more accurate accounting system for the violence; (b) better assessing the costs of reactive and proactive violence prevention efforts (or of neglect); (c) generating concrete suggestions to increase the accountability of people who benefit directly or indirectly from the violence; (d) highlighting the negative role of epistemic violence and senti-mental walls; (e) improving the banding of peace and peace research; and (f) guaranteeing the academic freedom and the quality of peace research and education. Let us now deal with each of these points in more detail: (a) Developing a more accurate and comprehensive system for violence monitoring and accounting: Today's databanks have three needs: (1) They need more reliable information about the numbers of people killed. For some conflicts and groups of victims, the data on people killed are rough and unreliable. There are first, second and third class victims. (2) They need information about the whole fabric of violence, including so-called sensitive or forbidden statistics, for example, about horizontal inequality in multi-ethnic countries. (3) They need data on the costs and benefits of violence. (b) Anticipating and comparing the costs and benefits of neglect and/or reactive or proactive violence prevention: This is a complex methodological problem of counterfactuals. Michael Brown and Richard Rosecrance (1999) made an important contribution toward what will be a continuing critical debate in the years to come. (c) Increasing the accountability of people who commit and/or profit from violence: If violence grieved everybody, it would have disappeared from the earth long ago. The problem is that for some people violence still pays off. Therefore it is of crucial importance to identify and name greedy people who profit from conflicts and make them more accountable for their deeds. (d) Exposing the epistemic violence and the senti-mental walls which inhibit the peace building process: This is very important because peace building takes place within an environment of power and competing interests and values. In such a context, knowledge is a strategic asset. People in power try to manipulate this knowledge by controlling the media, research funding, school curricula and the public opinion. (e) Improving the branding of peace and peace research (Reychler, 2000): One of the problems confronting the peace research community is the image of peace that they project. People choose for peace on the basis of their mental image of a possible and desirable future state of their living environment. This image can be as vague as a dream or as precise as a goal or mission statement. If peace advocates articulate a view of a realistic, credible and attractive future for people, a condition that is better in some ways than what now exists, then this image will be a goal that beckons and motivates people to pursue it. Not all people are enticed by the idea of peace. For some, the term peace has more negative than positive connotations. There are people in the European Community who take peace for granted. For them it is not a very important issue. Peace is banal and Luc Reychler 13 boring. It is not considered cool. Others do not like it because during the Cold War peace movements were misled and used by the Communist regimes. Peace can also be distrusted when promoted by conservative regimes to prevent structural changes. Throughout history, people have fought to get rid of Pax Romana, Pax Germanica, Pax Sovietica, Pax Niponica and other imposed peaces. The negative image of peace can also be derived from the fact that some so-called peace gurus or experts are peace quacks (in Dutch the word is paxzalver.) The association of peace with absolute pacifism tends to convey an image of passivity. For so-called 'realists' or 'cynics', peace is seen as an unrealistic and/or dangerous pursuit. Finally, people can become apprehensive when the 'peace' that someone is promoting is not defined clearly. Something certainly must be done to make the concept of peace more attractive. This could be accomplished by formulating clear and compelling definitions of peace; by differentiating different types of peace; by convincing people that one can forget sustainable development when no efforts are made to create a sustainable peace; by making people aware that there are 'limits to violence'; and by convincing them that peace building is a serious enterprise that requires courage, professionalism and creativity. How can the idea or ideal of sustainable peace building be disseminated more effectively? One could ask marketing specialists how to promote 'peace' as a product – how to give it 'sex appeal'. Perhaps they could give peace a chance. Even more important is the role of peace building leadership. The leaders must capture the attention of the people through a clear and compelling vision of peace. Such a vision is necessary to bridge the present and the future. A third group that can promote peace more effectively is the journalists. A distinction made by Johan Galtung (n.d.) between 'peace and conflict' journalism and 'war and violence ' journalism seems appropriate here. 'Peace and conflict' journalism could help to enhance the image of peace and peace-building significantly. Peace researchers must give serious consideration to the issue of the branding of peace and peace research. (f) Protecting the academic freedom and the quality of peace research and peace education: Academic freedom is of vital importance for peace researchers. Researching "truth" in conflict zones is a risky business. In a climate of political correctness, academic taboos, spin doctors, groupthink, embedded journalism and epistemic violence, the pressure to conform can be very high. An essential ingredient of sustainable peace building is professionalism and a critical mass of leaders who can raise hopes, generate ways and means to build peace, and commit people to the peace-building process. This necessitates not only peace building skills, but also the will to take some risks in order to achieve one's ends. Peace building is one of the fields of expertise in which there is no systematic control of the training and selection of people for conflict prevention and peace building functions. As a consequence, one finds peace quacks in the peace building sector. It's high time to have a discussion about the meaning of professionalism in peace building. The plea for more professionalism does not imply that professionals should be in charge of the peace building process. This would be unacceptable in a democratic 14 Challenges of Peace Research peace building process. Professionals, however, should help the people and the decision makers to make better informed decisions; they should make initial conflict impact assessments of the policies under consideration; and they should help generate more effective peace building alternatives. This has become the normal procedure in other fields, where health, employment, gender and environmental impact studies have become normal practice.*

CHAPTER SIX

How can we make peace

The United Nations was created in 1945, following the devastation of the Second World War, with one central mission: the maintenance of international peace and security. The UN accomplishes this by working to prevent conflict, helping parties in conflict make peace, deploying peacekeepers, and creating the conditions to allow peace to hold and flourish. These activities often overlap and should reinforce one another, to be effective.

The UN Security Council has the primary responsibility for international peace and security. The General Assembly and the Secretary-General play major, important, and complementary roles, along with other UN offices and bodies.

History has been proof of the thousands of wars that have taken place in all periods at different levels between nations. Thus, we learned that peace played an important role in ending these wars or even preventing some of them.

In fact, if you take a look at all religious scriptures and ceremonies, you will realize that all of them teach peace. They mostly advocate eliminating war and maintaining harmony. In other words, all of them hold out a sacred commitment to peace.

It is after thousands of destructive wars that humans realized the importance of peace. Earth needs peace in order to survive. This applies to every angle including wars, pollution, natural disasters, and more.

When peace and harmony are maintained, things will continue to run smoothly without any delay. Moreover, it can be a savior for many who do not wish to engage in any disrupting activities or more.

In other words, while war destroys and disrupts, peace builds and strengthens as well as restores. Moreover, peace is personal which helps us achieve security and tranquillity and avoid anxiety and chaos to make our lives better.

How to Maintain Peace

There are many ways in which we can maintain peace at different levels. To begin with humankind, it is essential to maintain equality, security, and justice to maintain the political order of any nation.

Further, we must promote the advancement of technology and science which will ultimately benefit all of humankind and maintain the welfare of people. In addition, introducing a global economic system will help eliminate divergence, mistrust, and regional imbalance.

It is also essential to encourage ethics that promote ecological prosperity and incorporate solutions to resolve the environmental crisis. This will in turn share success and fulfill the responsibility of individuals to end historical prejudices.

Similarly, we must also adopt a mental and spiritual ideology that embodies a helpful attitude to spread harmony. We must also recognize diversity and integration for expressing emotion to enhance our friendship with everyone from different cultures.

Finally, it must be everyone's noble mission to promote peace by expressing its contribution to the long-lasting well-being factor of everyone's lives. Thus, we must all try our level best to maintain peace and harmony.

1 Start by stamping out exclusion

Evidence shows that conflict happens in places where people can't trust the police or get access to justice, and their prospects for a decent life are stolen by corrupt elites. Governments everywhere need to stop the neglect, abuse, and stigmatization of their own people. Media and others that promote 'them-and-us' thinking must be challenged to stop spreading hate.

2 Bring about true equality between women and men

The larger a country's gender gap, the more likely it is to be involved in violent conflict, according to research in Valerie Hudson's Sex and World Peace (2012). Gender inequality trumps GDP, level of democracy, or ethnic-religious identity as the strongest push factor for both external and internal conflict more likely, and being the first to resort to force in such conflicts. In contrast, when women participate in peace processes, peace is more likely to endure.

3 Share out wealth fairly

Advert

According to a World Bank survey, 40 percent of those who join rebel groups do so because of a lack of economic opportunities. Relative poverty is just as important, with more equal societies marked by high levels of trust and low levels of violence. Economic fairness when it comes to public resources, taxation, and tax evasion is also key. The systematic transfer of wealth from rich to poor – instead of the other way around – improves security for everyone.

4 Tackle climate change

Ecological stress from global warming is proven to exacerbate conflicts over resources such as land and water, particularly in East Africa. For all its shortcomings, the UN climate agreement is evidence that the world can tackle and mitigate crises through co-operation, instead of war. A functioning climate deal 'is the greatest peace deal the world could have,' according to Dan Smith, from the leading arms-control thinktank SIPRI.

5 Control arms sales

The promotion of arms sales and heavy spending on aggressive military capabilities is heightening global tensions. The proliferation of arms drives conflict and makes violence more likely. Arms treaty signatories must be held to their word, as we build evidence of violations and hold sellers accountable. We can also build support for a groundbreaking new convention that bans nuclear weapons and makes it illegal to possess or use them.

6 Display less hubris, make more policy change

Advert

A look at the track record of counter-terrorism, the 'war on drugs', stabilization and state-building efforts, and colonial wars 'shows a pattern of largely very sobering failure' says Saferworld's Larry Attree. Humility and willingness to atone for past aggression on the international stage are essential – as is an end to the self-serving and counter-productive policy in the Middle East.

7 Protect political space

If governments expect young, marginalized people to embrace an open society rather than pursue more violent and vengeful paths, they must allow public dissent. Across the world – and the political spectrum – this space must be defended from repressive tools such as ad hoc administrative regulation, misuse of anti-terrorist measures, arbitrary arrest and imprisonment, and even torture and murder.

8 Fix intergenerational relations

Many conflicts can be understood as a youth revolt against established corrupt systems run by, generally, older men. In countries with strict age hierarchies young people can't voice their frustrations, which creates a dangerous dynamic, explains researcher and peacebuilder Chitra Nagarajan. This is compounded by classic victim-blaming, in which young men are treated as a ticking time bomb.

9 Build an integrated peace movement

Short-term anti-war movements have taken the place of active and permanent peace movements. We need to promote nonviolent alternatives and successes; peace campaigner Phyllis Bennis believes peace must be woven into other social movements, giving the example of the Poor People's Campaign in the US last March, which attacked the war economy and linked it to poverty at home.

10 Look within

Peace starts with you. Ordinary citizens can make a difference. When's the last time you said sorry? Think about who loses when you win. Are the people around you heard and respected or marginalized, ignored and left out? Make a decision to care about what happens to them. Start a constructive conversation with someone you disagree with. Challenge 'them-and-us' thinking in yourself as well as in others. Every one of us can choose to make society more just and peaceful, or more unjust and war-like.